The Book of Revelation:
The Seven Seals

by John Greg Stinson

And what is the exceeding greatness of His power toward us who believe, according to the working of His mighty power, which He worked in Jesus when He raised Him from the dead and seated Him at His right hand in the heavenly places.

The Book of Revelation:

The Seven Seals

Copyright 2022

Unless otherwise indicated, all Scripture quotations are taken from the Holy Bible King James Version.

All rights reserved

Published by

John Greg Stinson

The Book of Revelation:
The Seven Seals

Table of Contents

Introduction

The Holy Bible is the greatest book that has ever been written. Every word in the Holy Bible was written by God through Jesus, when Jesus had given revelation to men who were believers and men who were holy and obedient to Him. So, there are two kinds of people that are able to receive revelation from God through Jesus and those two people are: A person who believes and a person who is holy. Every holy person is a believe, but every believer isn't holy. Both people are capable of receiving revelation from Jesus. God has always given a believe revelation through words and the words Jesus had given the believer was written down, so that other believers would have the chance to learn the things that has to do with God. Throughout Christian history, God had always revealed things to people who were believers, through another person who is also, a believer. The believer that God reveals things to, is a believer that has a spirituality, that is much higher than the believers who is at the receiving end of the revelation. The person who is at the receiving end of the revelation of God, is the person who receives what God wants someone to know.

The person who God reveals something to, is the person who has the Heavenly spiritual intelligence to receive the knowledge that God wants to share with everyone who is a believer. Heavenly spiritual intelligence is known as, "discern" and it is a gift that comes from God, through Jesus, by the Holy Spirit. There are some people who can see God more than others. There are some people who believe more than others concerning the things of God. God reveals more to people who believe more and God reveals less to people who believe less. The more you believe, the more God will reveal things to you.

Throughout Christian history, there were certain people who were truly blessed by God; to learn something from God, that most people couldn't learn from God. That is something God has done throughout the existence of man. People are chosen by God to do certain things and receiving revelation to teach others is one of them.

God's purpose of giving people revelation is something that God had done in the Old Testament times and it is something that God also does in the New Testament times. The people who God gave revelation to in the Old Testament times, were called, "the Holy Prophets" and the people who God gave revelation to in the New Testament times were called, "the Holy Apostles."

It was through the Holy Prophets in the Old Testament times that people received revelation from God, concerning what God wanted people to do and also concerning the way they were expected by God to live their lives, but that wasn't the only thing God wanted the people of the Old Testament times to know: God especially, wanted people in Old Testament times to know about the coming of His Son Jesus. The coming of the Son of God was something that God wanted people to know in the Old Testament times; just as well as in the New Testament times.

Why? Because in the Old Testament times, salvation was just as important as it was in the New Testament times because the only way a person can receive eternal life is through salvation and the only way a person can receive salvation from God, is through Jesus. A person has to receive salvation first, before they can receive eternal life. Jesus is the person of the Godhead, that God the Father, did everything through in the Old Testament times, just as He did in the New Testament times; the only difference is, in the Old Testament times, Jesus was called, "the Word" in the Kingdom of God, before He was sent here to this earth as a man to die for the sins of men.

Everything mentioned in the Holy Bible, has everything to do with the return of Jesus, the Son of God because everything in the Holy Bible points to the return of Jesus, the Son of God. Like I said previously, God revealed things to people through other people who has the gift of discernment. The gifts of God are given to certain people who are on a certain level of belief and who are on a certain level of Heavenly living. All of the Holy Prophets and Apostles had the gift of discernment. Some gifts come from having other gifts. The gift of discernment comes from the gift of knowledge and the gift of wisdom comes from the gift of being able to understand, the knowledge that you received from God. Many people don't receive the gifts that comes from God, but the people who have always received the gifts that comes from God, are the "Holy Prophets and Apostles."

One believer, who received the gifts that comes from God, was the "Apostle John." The Apostle John, was the believer who wrote, "the book of Revelation." There are many theories about the Apostle John. I will tell you who the Apostle John was. The Apostle John did many things that aren't written in the Holy Bible. The Apostle John preached the Gospel of Jesus, the same time the Apostle Paul preached the Gospel of Jesus.

Out of all the Apostles, Paul was the Apostle that was the greatest among them all and other Apostles learned many things about Jesus from the Apostle Paul. Just like Paul, John was given something very special from Jesus and that was his spiritual ability to see many specific things that would happen in the future, that has everything to do with the return of Jesus. Out of all the holy people, who has ever lived here on this earth, the Apostle John was the holy person who saw the most. John was truly blessed by God, just like all of the other Apostles, to see specific things that would happen here on this earth, as a result of the coming of the Son of God. The Apostle John was one of the original twelve disciples of Jesus. John was also the Apostle, who experienced the great visitation from God, on the Mountain of Transfiguration; along with Peter and James. The Apostle John also wrote the books called, "the gospel of John and Revelation." There are four gospels; Matthew, Mark, Luke and John.

The Apostle John, just like other amazing Biblical writers, used things that people were familiar with on this earth during that time, to explain Heavenly situations and Jesus did the same thing as well. In chapter 6 of Revelation, which is the chapter I will explain; along with chapter 7 and the first part of chapter 8: I will explain some of the physical things John used to explain Heavenly situations. One of the physical things John used was the Scroll.

The Scroll: Back during the time of John, the scroll was used by Jewish leaders and the scroll was very important to Jewish leaders. Matter of fact, the only person who would write in and on a scroll was a Jewish leader. The only things a Jewish leader would write in a scroll, were things that had to do with the Kingdom of God: All other things a Jewish leader would write about were written on parchment paper, but not in the form of a scroll. Parchment paper was the kind of paper a scroll was made from during the time of John. When a Jewish leader would write something in a scroll, other Jewish leaders were allowed to read what was written in the scroll, but what the High Priest wrote in a scroll, was only for the High Priest and no one else was allowed to read what the High Priest wrote in a scroll. If someone was allowed to read what the High Priest wrote in a scroll, it was his assistant, who was called, "a curate" but he would respect the privacy of the High Priest and refuse to read what the High Priest wrote in the scroll.

The High Priest, along with other Jewish leaders who would write in and on a scroll, would write things on the inside of the scroll and also on the outside of the scroll. What was written on the inside of the scroll, was completely connected to what was written on the outside of the scroll. What the High Priest would write on the inside of the scroll, had to do with what he wanted to happen on the inside of the synagogue and what the High Priest wrote on the outside of the scroll had to do with what he wanted to happen on the outside of the synagogue, but both things were completely connected: What happened on the inside of the synagogue and what happened on the outside of the synagogue. In the same way, God the Father, just like the High Priest, writes things on a scroll and the only person who is qualified to read what is in the scroll, is Jesus because Jesus, is God the Father's assistant, just as the curate was the High Priest's assistant and just as the curate would respect the High Priest's privacy; Jesus respects the Father's privacy.

Just as the High Priest, along with other Jewish leaders: would write in a scroll; in the same way, God the Father writes in a scroll. God the Father writes on the inside and on the outside of the scroll, just as the High Priest would write on the inside and on the outside of the scroll. What is written in God scroll on the inside, is completely connected to what God wrote on the outside of the scroll. What God wrote on the inside of the scroll, has to do with how the new universe will function and what is written on the outside of the scroll has to do with how the new earth will function, but until then, no one knows: Not even Jesus, only the Father. So, when I hear preachers on television, saying things concerning what will happen on the new earth; they don't know because Jesus don't know and I heard some preachers on television, saying what they thought, concerning how people will live on the new earth and no one knows that, except the Father. The inside of the scroll is the new universe and the outside of the scroll is the new earth. When God decides to do something, it is recorded on parchment paper, just like when the High Priest decided to do something, it was recorded on parchment paper. When God decides to do something, that only He knows about, then the parchment paper becomes a scroll, just like when the High Priest decided to do something, that only he knew about, then the parchment paper became a scroll.

The Seals: During the time of John, when a Jewish leader wrote something in a scroll, he would place a seal on the scroll. The seal was a sign of privacy. The seal showed other people that no one had the right to read what was written in the scroll, unless they were permitted to. If there was something written in the scroll that a Jewish leader didn't want someone to know, then he would put a seal on the scroll.

There were also other scrolls that obtained important information that was available to other people, but those scrolls didn't have a seal. When a Jewish leader would take away the seal from the scroll, then that was a sign, that he would do what he had written in the scroll. Most scrolls didn't have a seal on them, but the scroll the High Priest wrote on, had a seal on them, but the information a High Priest would write in a scroll, was information the High Priest didn't want anyone to know, except him.

Like I said, when a Jewish leader would remove a seal from a scroll, he would do what he wrote in the scroll. The High Priest, was the only Jewish leader who wouldn't remove a seal from a scroll that he placed a seal on: His assistant would remove the seal; whereas, other Jewish leaders would remove the seal themselves from the scroll, they had written something important in. The High Priest, along with other Jewish leaders; had many scrolls that obtained different information. Unlike the Father, He has only one scroll and on that scroll are seven different seals and Jesus is the only person who is able to remove those seals, just like the High Priest's assistant, was the only person who could remove the seal from the High Priest's scroll. Because the seal was taken off the scroll, when the High Priest decided to do what he had written in the scroll, the seal represented something the High Priest would do, as preparation, for what he would do that was written in the scroll.

In the same way, Jesus will remove the seal, as preparation, for what He will do for God that is completely connected, to what He would do that has to do with His return. The seven seals that are on God's scroll represents each thing Jesus will do, that will make preparation for what Jesus would do for

God that is written in the scroll. Each seal, on God scroll represents something Jesus would do that has everything to do with what God wants to happen, that is mentioned on the inside and on the outside of the scroll. Jesus has to release the seals before He can do what is mentioned in the scroll. In other words, Jesus has to do what the seals represent before He can do what the inside and the outside of the scroll represents.

The Horses: Back during the time of John, just like today, there were many battles between different countries. On this earth, there were many battles between many countries. Back then, just like today; before a battle, the king would make preparations before he would go into battle against another country. There were a lot of preparations the king would make before a battle, but the first thing a king would do in preparation for a battle, is he would get his horses ready before anything else, so the horses were the first thing the king would get ready before the war.

As a result, when everyone would see the king preparing his horses, they knew for sure a war was about to happen, if they weren't familiar that a war was about to happen. The horses were the most important preparation a king would do towards a war. There have been many battles between God and humanity.

There are a lot of preparations God does before He goes to war with humanity, but the first thing God will do in preparation for a battle against humanity, is He will get His horses ready, which are "His Holy Angels."

The most important thing in the battles that God had against humanity, is His Holy Angels. The Holy Angels is what God uses when He goes to war with humanity. The reason why God's Holy Angels are called, "horses" is because His Holy Angels are used for the same principle, a king would use his horses for in battle, during the time of John. During the time of John, a king would use His horses to defeat another king, in the same way, God uses His Holy Angels to defeat humanity. From the beginning of humanity, God has always used His Holy Angels, as horses, to defeat a group of people He was going to war against. Sometimes, the defeat resulted in death and sometimes it didn't.

The Rider: Back during the time of John, every horse that was used in battle by a king had a soldier on it as the rider. The soldier, who was the rider, would be completely responsible for where the horse would go on the battle field. A soldier, on a horse in battle was very important. A horse in battle, needed a soldier to influence the horse where to go on the battle field, where other soldiers were located on the battle field, in whom the soldier on the horse, wanted to kill. It wouldn't make any sense for a king to send a horse on a battle field without a rider on it. Where a horse would go, regardless, if it was on a battle field or off a battle field, would depend on the influence of the rider. If a horse is either walking or running without a rider, then the horse would go where it wants to go, but if a horse has a rider on it, then it would go where the rider would influence it to go. A soldier on a horse in battle during the time of John, would influence the horse to go where the enemy soldiers would be.

In the same way, every Holy Angel that God's uses in battle against humanity has a soldier on it as the rider. The soldier who is the rider, is completely responsible for were the Holy Angel of God would go, as the Holy Angel is fighting a against humanity. The soldier is the influence, the Holy Angel receives from God, concerning where God wants that particular Angel to go, as the Angel is going to war against a group of people God is angry with. An Angel of God never comes here on this earth and roam around on his own.

Where ever an Angel of God goes to destroy those who God is angry with, that Angel is influenced by God to go where ever that Angel goes, but God is not the rider. The rider is the influence God has over the Angel, concerning where the Angel is supposed to be here on this earth to destroy, the people who God want to destroy because of His anger.

The influence God has over each Angel, through Jesus, is the soldier on the horse because God's influence is produced by He's divine skill, just like the soldier on the horse had amazing skill. It doesn't make sense for God to send an Angel without a soldier, which is once again, an influence. If God sends an Angel without influence, then that Angel can do what it wants to do, as the Angel is here on this earth. An Angel can never do what it wants to do, it has to do whatever God tells him to do through Jesus. If God sends an Angel here on this earth to fight against a group of people, then that Angel has to go to the people that God wants that Angel to destroy. When an Angel of God does what God wants, then that Angel is influenced by God to do whatever that Angel does for God. As a result, an Angel only destroys the people who God wants that particular Angel to destroy; an Angel never does anything on his own.

Everyone who is destroyed by God's Angel is an enemy of God and where ever God's enemies are here on this earth, that is where God will send His Angels. Where ever God sends His Angels, then that is where God will influence His Angels to go. The influence of God is very knowledgeable skill that completely controls His Angel: Not only where to go, but what to do, when they get to where God wants them to be. So, the horse is the Angel of God and the rider is what God will influence the Angel to do.

The Colors: The horses who are the Holy Angels of God have different colors. The colors have to do with what the Angel would do to people here on this earth, when the seals are released by Jesus at God's command. The colors of the horses represent what God will use His Angels to do, to the people here on this earth who He will destroy. Because the Angels are the spiritual beings God will use to destroy people here on this earth, that is the reason why the horses are different colors. As you read the book you will get an understand about the different colors of the horses. In this book, I will explain the sixth, seventh and some of the eightieth chapter of Revelation. These chapters are the main point of the book of Revelation. If a person is able to understand these chapters, then they are able to understand the book of Revelation.

In the 6th chapter and the 1st verse, in the King James version it says, **"Now I saw when the Lamb opened on of the seals; and I heard one of the four living creatures saying with a voice like thunder, "Come and see."** In the English version it says, **"Then I saw the Lamb break open the first of the seven seals, and I heard one of the four living creatures say in a voice that sounded like thunder, "Come!"**

Jesus is the only spiritual person in God's Kingdom that can break open the seven seals that are on God's scroll. It is through Jesus, the Son of God, that God does everything through. God created all things through Jesus. God created everything through Jesus because Jesus is the Holy Word of God and God does everything by speaking the Holy Word that comes forth from His Mouth. Jesus isn't only the Holy Word of God, but Jesus is the power of God. A person can only experience the power of God through Jesus. This is an example; your body is able to move through the energy your body produces when your body is physically active. The body produces energy, when the body is active and the energy the body produces, is seen by the physical things the body is able to do through the energy, the body produces within.

So, the energy the body produces is seen through the things the body does physically. In the same way, the power God produces is seen through the physical things Jesus does in a believer's life and the physical things Jesus does is seen through the Holy Spirit.

In the Kingdom of God, Jesus is not only recognized as the Holy Word of God, but after His crucifixion and death on the cross, Jesus was also known as the "Lamb of God." That was a name, that was given to Jesus by John the Baptist and it was a name that God the Father had accepted. Anything a holy person does and say is accepted by the Father and because it is accepted by the Father, it is also accepted by Jesus and the Holy Spirit because all three of these beautiful people agree with each other because all three of them have the same point of view. As I was saying, John the Baptist was the holy person who gave Jesus the name, "the Lamb of God." John the Baptist gave Jesus the name, "the Lamb of God" because John the Baptist knew that Jesus death on the cross had the same principle, as the protection that each Hebrew Israelite family received, when they put the blood of a Lamb on and over the door post of each house where a Hebrew Israelite family lived, during the time of the Passover, which was something that God had told the Hebrews to do through Moses.

The Passover, in Egypt; during the time of Moses, was an event that took place to protect each Hebrew family from the death Angel send by God, to kill every first-born male in Egypt. The blood of the Lamb was what protected every Hebrew family from the death Angel, as the death Angel Passed over Egypt; killing every Egyptian first-born male. Every house that had the blood of the Lamb on and over the door post was protected from the death Angel that passed over Egypt during the time of Moses. In the same way, every person who has the blood of Jesus on and over them, is protected by the death Angel that come from God's Kingdom and also from the demon death angel that is in the world. So, the people who have the blood of Jesus on and over them are protected from two kinds of death: Physical death and spiritual death. Physical death because they will live a long life that comes from the death that Jesus experienced on the cross and the spiritual death that separates a person's soul from the Spirit of God because of sin. Just as the blood of the Lamb protected the Hebrews, in the same way, the blood of Jesus protects a person who is cover under the blood of Jesus, **then I saw the Lamb.**

The only spiritual person in God's Kingdom who can break open the seals from off of God's scroll, is Jesus, the Son of God. In the first verse, of the sixth chapter of John, Jesus breaks open the first of the seven seals and the reason why John saw Jesus break open each seal, is because God had allowed for John to see many of the things that would happen, by His Angels, in the coming future. As John saw Jesus break open each seal, John saw the things that would happen in the future that each seal represents. Different things will happen as Jesus removes each seal and John was truly blessed to see those things happen that the seals represent, many years before they happen. A person is blessed by God, if God shows them things He will do before they happen and John was one of those people who was truly blessed by God, to see many things that God was going to do, although, He hadn't done them during the time He revealed them to John. Jesus is the spiritual person in God's Kingdom who will causes those things to happen, that God wants to happen, before He sends His Son Jesus, **break open the first of the seven seals.**

In God's Kingdom, there are many Angels. Matter of fact, there are more Angels then there are people here on this earth. All of God's Angels have different positions and as a result, some Angels are higher than other Angels. The two groups of Angels in God's Kingdom that are the highest of all of God's Angels, are the Cherubim Angels and the Seraphim Angels. The Cherubim Angels are the highest Angels in God's Kingdom and there are only four of them.

The second group of Angels that are the second highest in God's Kingdom, are the Seraphim Angels and there are only seven of them. These two groups of Angels aren't principalities like many people in the church think. These two groups of Angel are far beyond the position of principalities and any other Angels in God's Kingdom. The Angels that reveals God's anger through the noise of thunder are the Cherubim's. No other Angel in God's Kingdom does that, except the Cherubim. Whenever a Cherubim speaks in a voice that sounds like thunder, then that means God is angry and not long after that voice, something will happen to the people who God is angry with, **I heard one of the four living creatures say in a voice that sounded like thunder.**

Like I said earlier, John was truly blessed to see the things God had shown him, concerning the things He would do here on this earth, to the people He was angry with. After the Cherubim's got John's attention through the Holy Spirit, then the Angel showed John the things that God was going to do to the people here on this earth because of His Anger, **Come.**

In the 2nd verse, in the King James version it says, **And I looked, and behold, a white horse. He who sat on it had a bow; and a crown was given to him, and he went out conquering and to conquer.** In the English version is says, **I looked and there was a**

white horse. Its rider held a bow and he was given a crown. He rode out as to conqueror to conquer.

Through the Holy Spirit, one of the Cherubim Angels was able to show John many Angels, but the first group of Angels John saw after the Cherubim Angels, were the Seraphim Angels and the reason why John was able to see those Angels as well, was because they were the Angels that would release God's anger, on the people who lived here on this earth, who God was angry with during the time of John's vision. The first Seraphim Angel John saw was the Seraphim Angel that represented a white horse. The reason why the first Seraphim Angel was white, is because of the kind of people he would be assigned to defend. The people who this Seraphim Angel would be assigned to defend were the people who were on this earth who were holy.

Holiness represents white because white is a color that is pure, which means, it isn't mixed with any other color to take away its purification. The people who the first Seraphim Angel would protect were the people who were holy and the Angel would protect them from people who were unholy **and I looked, and behold, a white horse.** The first Angel, who was the white horse, was not only assigned by God to protect the people who were holy, but to harm the people who had harmed them.

When God sends an Angel to punish a person or a group of people, the punishment doesn't always result in death, sometimes the punishment results in injury. When people mistreat and harm other people who are holy; God will punish them as a result. That was the assignment given to the Angel by God that represented the color white. Harming, but not killing, those who mistreated and harmed the people who were holy, is what the "white horse Angel" was influenced to do by God and that was the reason why the Angel did it, **he who sat on it had a bow.**

Out of the seven Seraphim Angels, the Seraphim that represented the color white, was the Seraphim that had the most authority and power than the rest of the seven Seraphim. The reason why, is because it would be this Angel that God would use to create everything over again and make everything new. This Angel won't destroy the old, but he will create the new, after the old is destroyed. So as a result, the Angel that represents the white horse; he has the most authority and power than the rest of the seven Seraphim, **and a crown was given to him.**

All of God's Angels win the war they are sent to fight for God. Losing is not an option. When an Angel come here on this earth to fight for God, they will fight only for the purpose of winning and as they fight, they will fight, the fight they are fighting until they have won.

The first Seraphim Angel that will come here to this earth to fight against the people who are and will mistreat and harm God's holy people; he will win against those people as he is fighting them and he will continue to fight them until he wins and defeat them, **and he went out conquering and to conquer.** If you notice I said who are. The reason why I said that is because the first, second, third and fourth seal already happened.

In the 3rd verse, in the King James version is says, **when he opened the second seal, I heard the second living creature saying, "come and see."** In the English version is says, **when the Lamb broke the second seal, I heard the second living being say, come!"**

Like I said earlier, Jesus is the person who breaks open the seals because He is the person who will give the Seraphim Angels the command to do what the seals represents that has everything to do with His return. At the time of John's vision, the only people in God's Kingdom that was able to see what would happen in the future, that the seven seals represent, was and is, the Father, Jesus, the Holy Spirit and the Cherubim Angels. That's the reason why the Cherubim Angels were able to show John the things that would happen here on this earth that the seven seals represent.

The reason why the Cherubim Angels were the only Angels that can see what God would do in the future, that the seven seals represent, is because they are the Angels who will be over all the Angels, through the Seraphim Angels and the Seraphim Angels will be over all the Angels, who will help them do what God wants to be done here on this earth at the very end of time. The reason why the four Cherubim Angels are called, "creatures" is because they are different from all the other Angels that are in God's Kingdom and the reason why they are different, is because of the power and authority they have over all other Angels. The Cherubim Angels are the only Angels that are around God's throne. So, they are the Angels that are directly in the presence of the Father and Jesus.

In the 4th verse, in the King James version it says, **another horse, fiery red, went out. And it was granted to the one who sat on it to take peace from the earth and that people should kill one another; and there was given to him a great sword.** In the English version it says, **another horse came out, a red one. Its rider was given the power to bring war on the earth, so that people should kill each other. He was given a large sword.**

If an Angel of God is sent here to this earth, he is sent here to this earth to either bless or punish. If an Angel is sent here to this earth to bless, then they will bless the people who God is pleased with. If they are sent here on this earth to punish, then they will punish the people who God isn't pleased with. Like I said earlier, sometimes Angels are sent here to punish by harming someone, which will result in wounding and sometimes they are sent to kill. The punishment given by God through an Angel can result in harm or death. In the first verse, of chapter six, the Angel was sent to harm by wounding; in this verse, the Angel was sent to kill. When a person is killed by another person, it always results in the pouring out of a lot of blood. So in other words, when a person kills another person, the person who is killed, will lose a lot of blood because when a person kills another person out of anger and rage, they kill the person in such a way that the person who is killed will bleed out a lot, **another horse, fiery red, went out.**

So, there is blood everywhere when a person is killed. In most cases, this kind of killing is done when a person is angry and furious towards another person or in a time were a war in going on between two or more countries.

This is the kind of killing; the second Seraphim will cause. This Angel will cause this kind of killing on the battle field and off the battle field, when he will influence people to do what is right that would enrage and make other people very upset who represents and stand up for what is wrong. This will influence demons to work on people more, which will influence many countries to go to war with other countries and influence many people to violently kill other people because of rage and anger, **and it was granted to the one who sat on it to take peace from the earth and that people should kill one another.** As a result, many people will be killed in a violent way on the battle field and off the battle field and I mean a lot and that is seen today because this seal has already been broke off the scroll by Jesus along with the first seal. As we see today, many people are being killed in a violent way and I mean many people, **there was given to him a great sword.** Like I said earlier, the first, second, third and four seal has already been released from the scroll of God by Jesus, but not the fifth, sixth and seventh seal.

In the 5th and 6th verse, in the King James version it says, **when He opened the third seal, I heard the third living creature say, Come and see." So, I looked and behold, a black horse, and he who sat on it had a pair of scales in his hand. And I heard a voice in the midst of the four living creatures saying, "A quart of wheat for a denarius and three**

quarts of barley for a denarius; and do not harm the oil and the wine. In the English version it says, **when the Lamb broke the third seal, I heard the third living creature say, "Come!" I look up and saw a black horse, and its rider was holding a pair of scales in his hand. And I heard a voice from among the four living beings say, "A loaf of wheat bread or three loaves of barley will cost a day's pay. And don't waste the olive oil and wine."**

When a person receives revelation from God, the revelation they receive come from above, which is from God's Kingdom. The reason why the revelation a person receives from God comes from above is because God's Kingdom is up from where the earth and everything else in the universe is located. So, when a person receive revelation from God here on this earth, the revelation they receive comes from above because above is where God's presence is because above, which is up, is where God's lives, **I look up.**

The opposite of black is white. Black represents evil and wickedness and white represents holiness and pure. The Angels of God always represent what is holy and pure and reject what is evil and wicked. As a result, the Angels of God represent what is just and fair. Anything that is just and fair is equally balanced, just like the scale that is held in the hand of the Angel that represents the black horse.

Because the Angels of God are just and fair, they represent what is holy and pure and they reject what is evil and wicked. They have that kind of character because they have the character of God and God is always just and fair because He is a God that represents justice. If a person is holy and pure, they represent what is just and fair, just like God does, but if a person is evil and wicked, they represent what is wrong and unjust. People who are holy are fair like God and people who are wicked are unjust like the devil.

Most people, who have power over other people, are people who are black inside, which means, they are people who are evil and wicked. Throughout human history, most people who have power over other people, are unjust, toward the people, they have power over and throughout human history, most people have power over other people who are their employees. When slavery ended, black people would get paid for the work they did for a white slave master, but in most cases, the pay was unfair, which means that the employee was well under paid by their employer and a unfair wage not only happened between white employers and black employees, but it happened to everyone who was being paid by a particular employer. Throughout human history, employers have been known to be unfair to their employees concerning paid wages.

Why? Because throughout human history, more people who hired other people to work for them were black inside. As a result, it always resulted in unfair paid wages. Most people in the work world are under paid for the work they were hired to do and there is nothing they can do about it, but complain and there complaining doesn't solve a thing.

Employer who are unfair to their employees represent a scale that is unbalanced, unlike the scale that is held in the hand of the Angel of God that represents the black horse. God wants every employer to be fair with their employees, which is something that many employers failed to do in the past, during the time of John and also today. The Angel of God that represents the black horse is against all of the people who are employers who under pay their employees because the Angels of God are fair and just; just like God, **a black horse, and he who sat on it had a pair of scales in his hand.**

When God is very upset about something, He says something directly from His own mouth without speaking through an Angel, **and I heard a voice in the midst of the four living creatures saying.** God will become very upset when people who are employers, cheat other people who are their employees.

That is something that makes God very angry. The work world was different during the time of John, then it is today and what I mean by that is; back during the time of John, people worked for food, rather than for money. Today, people work for money, rather than for food. The food that people worked for during the time of John was wheat bread and bread made from barley, but the employers never gave their employees, the bread they should have received because of the work they did, which lasted all day, **a loaf of wheat bread or three loaves of barley will cost a day's pay.**

A loaf of wheat bread and three loaves of barley was the amount of food a person was expected to be paid, if they worked all day long, but most employees, back during the time of John, were paid a lot less bread then what they actually received and that made God very angry. The color black represents all the employers who are unfair with their paid wages. Believe me when I say this; all of the employers who were unfair and unjust in their wages were punished by God, when God cause them to go out of business. That is the reason why a lot of companies went out of business in the past. It was the Angel that represent the black horse who did that.

Although, most employers are unfair in their paid wages, there are some employers who are fair in their paid wages and they are the employers who hold in their hand, the same kind of scale that the Angels of God hold in their hand and it is a balanced scale. God never punished an employer who is fair to their employees concerning paid wages. An employer who is holy, which is an employer who is always joyful and happy, is the kind of employer the Angel of God doesn't punish, **and don't waste the olive oil and wine.**

In the 7th and 8th verse, in the King James version it says, **when He opened the fourth seal, I heard the voice of the fourth living creature saying, "Come and see." So, I looked and behold, a pale horse. And the name of him who sat on it was Death and Hades followed with him. And power was given to them over a fourth of the earth, to kill with sword, with hunger, with death and by the beasts of the earth.** In the English version it says, **then the Lamb broke open the fourth seal; and I heard the fourth living creature say, "Come!" I looked and there was a pale colored horse. Its rider was named Death and Hades followed close behind. They were given authority over one fourth of the earth, to kill by means of war, famine, disease and wild animals.**

The Angels of God are assigned by God to do many different things here on this earth. Most Angels are assigned by God to do things that relates to Salvation and other Angels are assigned by God to do things that are related only to the return of Jesus. The Angels that are assigned by God, to do something for God, they don't do alone, what they have been assigned by God to do, but the Angel that was given the assignment, is the Angel that is in charge of the rest of the Angels, that will help him do, what God has assigned for him to do. Some Angels are assigned to bless and some Angels are assigned to kill. The Cherubim Angel that represents the red horse, is assign to kill, just like the pale Cherubim Angel is assigned to kill, but both Angels are assigned to kill in a different way. The Cherubim Angel that represents the red horse is assigned to kill indirectly and the Cherubim Angel that represents the pale horse is assigned to kill directly.

All of God's Angels are holy, so they have the same good and righteous character God has, so the Angels of God are peaceful spiritual people, but through God's anger, they can be influenced by God, to kill those who God is angry with because of sin, but the Angels of God are good people. People are completely different in skin color when they are alive, compared to when they are dead. A person's skin color changes after a person have been dead for quite some time.

When a person is dead for a certain number of days, their skin color changes to a pale color, **a pale horse.** When people die in a country that has an excellent system of doing away with the dead, bodies don't lay around for a certain number a day until they are buried, so in the countries that have an excellent system of burying people, dead people are buried not long after they die. When that is the case, people who are alive, don't see the change in skin color that happens when a person is dead for a certain number of days. But a lot of foreign countries have a bad system of burying people and as a result, people who are alive; they see the change that happens in a person's skin color because they have been dead for a certain number of days.

This kind of death happens directly by an Angel of God, which means, it was the Angel who was responsible for whatever it was that happened that caused a person's death, which is the reason why the word death, in the eighth verse is capitalized, **Death.** There are certain ways the Angels of God kills people and the way that people are killed, in the eighth verse, is the way the Angel of God kills people. If an Angel kills someone, then most of the time, the person isn't buried quickly and when that happens, the change of a person's skin color is seen very clearly.

There are some deaths that results in a person's soul being carried to the lake of fire and the deaths that are caused by an Angel of God are the kinds of deaths that result in a person's soul being carried away to the lake of fire. So, if an Angel of God kills someone, then most likely that person's soul will end up in the lake of fire, **and Hades followed with him.**

When an Angel of God is assigned to kill some, by the command of God, that Angel is allowed to kill only a certain number of people. In some cases, Angels are allowed to kill more people than others. Today, Angels are allowed to kill only a small amount of people, **and power was given to them over a fourth of the earth.** But there will come a time when an Angel of God will be given the authority to kill many more people than a fourth. Like I said, the Angel of God kills people in certain ways that is different from the way that demons kill people. The Angel of God kills people, **by means of war, famine, disease and wild animals.** If a person is killed by Angel of God in these four ways, then most likely their souls ended up in the lake of fire because the lake of fire is where a person's soul will go, if they are killed by Angel.

In the 9th 10th and 11th verse, in the King James version it says, **when He opened the fifth seal, I saw under the altar the souls of those who had been slain for the Word of God and for the testimony which they held. And they cried with a loud voice, saying, How long, O Lord, holy and true, until You judge and avenge our blood on those who dwell on the earth? Then a white robe was given to each of them and it was said to them that they should rest a little while longer, until both the number of their fellow servants and their brethren, who would be killed as they were, was completed.**

In the English version it says, **then the Lamb broke open the fifth seal, I saw underneath the altar the souls of those who had been killed because they had proclaimed God's Word and had been faithful in their witnessing. They shouted in a loud voice, "Almighty Lord, holy and true! How long will it be until you judge the people on earth and punish them for killing us? Each of them was given a white robe and they were told to rest a little while longer, until the complete number of other servants and believers were killed as they had been.**

In the Old Testament times, there were some people who were killed for proclaiming to people, the message of God, that God wanted people to know at that particular time. The people who were killed in the Old Testament times for proclaiming God's message were the, "Holy Prophets of God."

The people who killed the Holy Prophets in Old Testament times, killed the Prophets because the message they gave to the people, which came from God, was a message that told them about their sins. If you want to make enemies, tell people about themselves, concerning the things they do that are wrong. If they repent, then you gained a friend, but if they refuse to repent, then you gained an enemy. All the Holy Prophets in the Old Testament times made enemies from the people they proclaimed the message of God to because the people didn't want to repent, after the message was given to them that came from God. After the Holy Prophets made enemies, by proclaiming God's message to the people, who didn't want to repent, then they were mistreated before they were killed. That kind a treatment continued into the New Testament time. In the same way, in the New Testament times, the holy people experienced the same kind of treatment, the Holy Prophets experienced in the Old Testament times.

In both ages, there were people here on this earth who proclaimed God's message to the people who God wasn't pleased with. In the New Testament times, there were many more people who were killed for proclaiming God's message, than there were in the Old Testament times and the principle was the same, which was anger that produced enemies for the people who was at the end of the anger. Holy people have always been at the end of the anger of people who weren't God's people, although, they claimed they were God's people. People of God don't fight against other people who are also people of God. Only people of the devil fight against the people of God.

In the past, holy people were always killed in a different way then worldly people. Holy people have always been slain, which is when a person is killed, as though, they were an animal. After a holy person is killed, their souls go to a different place, from the place a person soul goes who is a sinner. Every holy person's soul goes to Heaven, which is also called, "the Kingdom of God." When a person's soul goes to Heaven, it goes to a particular place in Heaven and that place is a place in God's Kingdom where the presence of God is. The presence of God the Father and Jesus, is in the part of the Kingdom of God, where God's throne is located and what I mean, when I said God's throne, is the place in His Kingdom where He rules.

The place in God's Kingdom, where He rules, is called, "His throne." God's presence exists outside of His Kingdom through the Holy Spirit. In front of the place, where God rules and control all things, is a spiritual object that is called, "an altar." Some physical building here on this earth are structured and built exactly like God's Temple and the tent, that God told Moses to build was one of those structures, that was exactly like God's Temple, which is where His throne is in Heaven. When a holy person's soul goes to Heaven, that person's soul goes to a spiritual place in God Temple, that is known as, "an altar."

The altar of God is only for the people who are holy here on this earth. It is only for those people that God created the altar in His Kingdom for, which is the reason why the altar was created here on this earth. So, the holy people are the subject of God's altar because they were the reason why God created the altar, **I saw under the altar the souls.** Just like animals were sacrificed on the altar here on earth, in the same way, holy people were sacrificed like animals, when they were killed like animals. Holy people were killed like animals for preaching the Word of God and for living their lives by the testimony of Jesus, **souls of those who had been slain for the Word of God and for the testimony which they held.**

The testimony of Jesus is the crucifixion and resurrection of Jesus and when a person does in their lives, what the crucifixion and resurrection of Jesus represents, they live their lives by the testimony of Jesus.

When a person dies, they are still able to do some of the things they did when they were here on this earth in bodily form. Some of the things a person is able to do when they die is: See, hear, smell, taste, feel and talk, which are all of the things a person is able to do when they are alive on this earth, it's just when they die, they aren't in bodily form, but they are still able to do some of the things they did when they were in bodily form. One of the main things a person can still do when they go to God's Kingdom after they die is; "talk." Most of the time, in God's Kingdom, people's souls talk to one another, but some time their souls talk to God. When people's souls talk to God in Heaven, they talk to God out of stress and if they ask God for something out of stress, God will give them what they asked Him for. When a person asks for something under stress, they may ask in a tone of voice that is much higher, than a tone of voice, they speak with in a regular tone of voice.

When a person asks another person for something under stress, their voice is much more louder damaging and straight forward, **they shouted in a loud voice, "Almighty Lord.** Whatever a person asks for under stress, that is what they want immediately, without delay.

The souls of the people who had been killed here on this earth because of Jesus, they wanted God to acted very quickly toward those people here on this earth who had killed them, which means that a person's soul who goes to Heaven, is still cautious of the things that happen here on this earth, that is why those people who were in Heaven, knew that the people who had killed them were still alive on this earth.

This is something that didn't happen yet, but will happen in the future. The past only becomes the future, when the same thing that happened in the past, happens again in the future. Just as people were killed in the past for Jesus, people will also be killed in the future for Jesus, during this time of John's vision of the future. So, a person can still become stress and frustrated when they are in soul spiritual form. Stress and frustration will cause a person to ask another person questions.

People have been known to ask even God questions during stressful and frustrating times and God will answer, the questions, of the people who are holy, **how long will it be until you judge the people on earth and punish them for killing us?**

In the eyes of God, people who are holy represent the color white because the color white represents purity and purity is when something isn't mixed with something else that is different from what already exist. A person who is holy; their soul isn't mixed with sin. Sin is different from what causes a person's soul to be holy and if a person's soul is mixed with sin, then a person's soul isn't holy, but defiled. When a person's soul is holy, then that person receives a position of priesthood because that is the kind of person who can get a pray through to God.

In the eyes of God, a holy person is recognized by God as a priest. In the eyes of God, a priest is identified as a person whose garment is a robe, just as a priest's garment in the Old Testament times was a robe. If a person wore a robe in the Old Testament times, then that person was easily identified as a priest. In the same way, if a person is wearing a robe that was given to him by God, then the person is easily identified by God as a priest.

God is the only person who can qualify someone with a robe and the person God qualify with a robe is holy in the eyes of God, **each of them was given a white robe.**

During this time of John's vision, which is something that didn't happen during John's time and it hasn't happened yet: Many people will be killed for Jesus sake. Just as it has always been; killing someone is a sin and every sin doesn't go unpunished. Everyone who commits sin will be punished by God, but those who kill people because they represent Jesus, will die a terrible death.

When a group of people are killed for the sake of Jesus, a certain number of them had to be killed before God will take His revenge against those who killed them. God knows how many people are killed for Jesus sake and because God knows how many people are killed for Jesus sake, during the time of John's vision, God won't take revenge against those people until the number of people are complete who supposed to die for Jesus sake. After everyone is killed for Jesus, that adds up to the number of people who are supposed to die for Jesus; during the time of John's vision, then God will kill those people who killed His servants, **and they were told to rest a little while longer, until the complete number of other servants and believers were killed as they had been.**

This is something that many servants of Jesus had experienced in Christian history, but what John's saw in his vision didn't happen yet.

In the 12th verse, in the King James version it says, **I looked when He opened the sixth seal and behold, there was a great earthquake and the sun became black as sackcloth of hair and the moon became like blood.** In the English version it says, **and I saw the Lamb break open the sixth seal. There was a violent earthquake and the sun became black like coarse black cloth and the moon turned completely red like blood.**

The presence of God is very powerful. The earth has always experienced the presence of God ever since God create man. There were many people here on this earth in the past who didn't realize when the earth experienced the presence of God. There has been and there will always be signs here on earth, that will let people know when God's presence is close to the earth. The signs, that all people have noticed in the past, that had to do with the presence of God, were signs that people thought would happen as a coincidence, other than the real reason why those signs actually happened. There were a lot of things that happened here on this earth that people thought happened as a coincidence, but they only happened because of God's presence.

God has to show a person when He is present. If God doesn't show a person when He is present, then it is impossible for a person to realize when He is present. God's presence will show a person when He is happy or sad and God will show a person that through a gift that God will give to those who believe and that gift is the gift of discernment. The gift of discernment will not only let a person know when God is present, but the gift of discernment will let a person know when God is happy or sad. There are certain signs that comes from God that will allow for a person to know if God is happy or sad. There were many people who were here on this earth in the past who recognized the signs that came from God.

Not all people who have come here on this earth were ignorant to the signs that God's presence reveals. There are signs that will show how happy God is and there are signs that will show how angry God is. God has emotions just like we do; the only difference is, God's emotions are divine and our emotions aren't divine. The signs that show God's happiness are good weather, the growing of food, the blooming of flowers, the absence of clouds, the purification of water or clean water and the absence of destructive land. The signs that show God's anger are the presence of clouds, the presence of storms, the presence of dirty water, the non-growing of food, the non-growing of flowers:

When I say, the non-growing of flower, I don't mean the flowers people plant around their homes or on their land, but flowers that grow in places where people don't plant or live. Two more signs that shows God's anger are the presence of destructive land and an **earthquake.**

There are signs that show God's different levels of happiness and there are signs that show God's different levels of anger. Some signs show how much God will bless a person and some signs will show how much God will punish a person and there are some signs that shows that God will punish a person, if they don't take heed to the good life that He wants everyone to live. There is only one sign God uses to show that He will punish, if people don't take heed to His commands and it is a sign that have always gotten peoples full attention, then other signs from God and that sign is an **earthquake.**

The reason why an earthquake will get a person's attention, much more than a storm, is because an earthquake is something the body can feel in an instant. If you see a tornado in a distance coming your way, you will see the tornado before you feel the impact of the tornado. In the case of an earthquake, you will feel the impact of an earthquake instantly.

So, an earthquake is a catastrophe God uses to get people's attention before punishment and all other earth catastrophes, God uses to get people's attention after punishment. Towards the end of all things, here on this earth, which will be just before the coming of Jesus, God will use a few earthquakes to get the attention of people and the earthquake that is mentioned in the twelfth verse, is the first great earthquake people will feel here on this earth, but there hasn't been any earthquakes this powerful yet. This kind of earthquake will be felt all over the world very plainly. The earthquakes we have today on this earth, are earthquakes that are mainly felt in the geographical area where the earthquake happened and there are some other geographical areas that will feel the same earthquake that happened somewhere else, but vaguely.

The kind of earthquake that is mentioned in the twelfth verse, is the kind of earthquake that will be felt all over the world, just as strong as it will be felt where the earthquake took place. The earthquake, in the twelfth verse, will be the first earthquake of that kind.

God has the power to do anything He wants to do. Even if it is impossible to do. God can do things that hasn't never been known to be done here on this earth. God can do things here on this earth that will make everyone sad and depressed.

Like I said earlier, God has signs that will show people His happiness and His anger. Everyone who experience the signs of God that shows His happiness; they will be happy, just as God is happy, but everyone who experience the signs of God that shows His anger; than everyone will be sad, just as God is sad. God is never happy when He punishes someone. The more people God punishes, the sadder He becomes, but it won't stop Him from doing what He is supposed to do. If a person is good, then they deserved to be blessed, but if a person is bad, then they deserved to be punished.

There will come a time when more people on this earth will be punished by God than ever before. When that happens, only God's anger is what the earth will experience and as a result, everyone who will be here on this earth during that time, who isn't faithful to God; they will experience difficult and very rough times here on this earth. During this time, most people will lose their lives by being killed, rather than by dying. There is a different when a person dies, than when they are killed. When a person dies, they lose their lives by their own hand, but if a person dies because they are killed, then they lose their lives by the hand of someone else or because something happened on this earth that created an impact that was capable of taking a person's life.

During this time in earthly history, most people will die by being killed. The number a death that will take place here on this earth, during this time, will cause everyone on this earth to be sad and depress. This will happen because of God's anger; **the sun became black.** This level of God's anger will cause everyone to go through rough times, **as sackcloth.** During the time of John, people made sackcloth out of hair because it was much more durable and it lasted much longer.

Before that, sackcloth was made from flax, which is a plant that can produce a rough fabric, but the sackcloth made with hair lasted a lot longer, then the sackcloth made from flax. The people who will be here on this earth during this time, will experience rough times like never before. So, during this time on this earth, it will be rough for people, then all the rough times people had experienced here on this earth in the past, **of hair.** Just like sackcloth made with hair was rougher than sackcloth made from flax, **of hair.**

Like I said, during this time, many people will be killed and because of that, there will be blood all over the earth. So much blood will pour out of people that there won't be enough people to clean it up, so blood will be visible everywhere on earth, **the moon became like blood.** Let me make something clear:

The sun will stop shining and the moon will be red like blood, but when the sun stops shining and the moon will look red like blood, that will represent the rough times people will go through on this earth and the amount of blood the earth will be covered with.

In the 13th verse, in the King James version it says, **and the stars of heaven fell to the earth, as a fig tree drops its late figs when it is shaken by a mighty wind.** In the English version it says, **the stars fell down to the earth, like unripe figs falling from the tree when a strong wind shakes it.**

God created all things in the universe through Jesus. There are some many celestial bodies in the universe; not even scientist, who study the stars, know how many celestial bodies there are. They can't come close to a number. In the universe, there are so many of the same celestial bodies and all the celestial bodies aren't in the same place in the universe, but they all have the same function, if they are the same celestial bodies, although, they aren't located in the same part of the universe. Just like there is a sun in our galaxy, there are many other suns, in many other galaxies that exist in the universe.

The sun is called, "the sun" in our galaxy because we are able to see the full capacity of what the sun does, which is to shine light, but all the other suns that are outside of our galaxy, are visible to our eyes as we look up in the sky, but because we can't see the full shining capacity of those suns; those suns are stars.

The suns in the universe will be the only celestial bodies that will fall from where they are in the universe and travel down toward to the earth at speeds that will be extreme to measure. The reason why the suns will drop down to the part of the universe where we are, is because where we are, is the end of the universe going down.

It's just like, if you would drop something from off the table: It will fall down to the floor because the floor is where the end is from the table. The suns, which in the thirteenth verse are called, "stars" will be the only celestial bodies that will be shaken from its place by God and everything else will remain in the universe where it belongs, **and the stars of heaven fell to the earth.** When those suns get to where we are, they will no longer be suns or stars, but meteors. A meteor is a much smaller version of any very large celestial body and those meteors will be a much smaller version of the suns, which are stars, that will fall to this part of the universe.

It is very easy for God to do anything that we see as being extremely hard because God has all power. When God removes the suns, in other parts of the universe, it will be something that will be very easy for Him to do. The size of the universe to God, is like what an ant or a fly is to us and much smaller than that. So, it will be very easy for God to remove the suns from where they are in the universe and make them fall here, in this part of the universe, **as a fig tree drops its late figs when it is shaken by a mighty wind.** This will be amazing to see because none of the stars will hit the earth. Have you ever seen a movie that had many meteors dropping down to the earth and none of those meteors hit the earth, well that is how it will be during the time of John's vision: This phenomenon is called, "a meteor shower."

In the 14th verse, in the King James version it says, **then the sky receded as a scroll when it is rolled up and every mountain and island was moved out of its place.** In the English version it says, **the sky disappeared like a scroll being rolled up and every mountain and island was moved from its place.**

Everything here on this earth will go back to the way in used to be when Adam was created by God, but there are somethings here on this earth that will go back to the way it used to be before Jesus returns.

When God created Adam, it didn't rain because there were no clouds in the sky and that is what will happen during the time, when God will make the suns leave from where they are located, in another part of the universe. The removing of the suns and the disappearing of the clouds will happen around the same time. The reason why God will get rid of the clouds, is because that will be a sign that God wants everyone to live, the way Adam lived, before he sinned. When Adam had a relationship with God, it didn't rain because there was no need for rain. The reason why there was no need for rain, is because God cause the earth to produce food directly, without using something. But that wasn't the primary reason why clouds didn't exist back before Adam had sinned.

The reason why the clouds didn't exist before Adam sinned, is because God wanted Adam to be able to see His presence from where he was on the earth at that time, which was in the Garden of Eden. God will remove the clouds again for the same reason, so that people on this earth can see His presence; as His presence approaches the earth to destroy the earth. So Adam was allowed to see God's presence because he had peace with God, but the people will see the presence of God here on this earth, during the time of the fourteenth verse because they will be at war with God and they will see God's presence, just like Adam was able to see God's presence, but for a different purpose, **the sky disappeared like a scroll being rolled up.**

During the time of Adam or before Adam sinned, the earth was perfect in shape, so there were no hills or mountains. During the time of Adam, all the land that was on the earth was together, so the earth was one big piece of land that had large streams of water running through it. Mountains and islands came into existence because of Adams sin. After Adam had sinned, the devil was able to interfere with the structure and form of the earth. The structure and form of the earth, the devil tampered with was the structure and form that is underneath the earth and that changed the way the earth was formed on the surface. When this happened, mountains and islands were created. Just like mountains and islands were created, God will uncreate them, **every mountain and island was moved from its place.** Why? Because it will be a sign, which will be ignored, that God wants people to be the same way Adam was before he sinned.

In the 15th 16th and the 17th verse, in the King James version it says, **and the kings of the earth, the great men, the rich men, the commanders, the mighty men, every slave and every free man, hid themselves in the caves and in the rocks of the mountains and said to the mountains and rocks, Fall on us and hide us from the face of Him who** sits on the throne and from the wrath of the Lamb. For the great day of His wrath has come and who will be able to stand? In the English version it says, **then the kings of the earth, the rulers and the military chiefs, the rich and the powerful and all other people, slave and free, hid themselves in caves and under rocks on the mountain. They called out to the mountains and to the rocks, "Fall on us and hide us from the eyes of the one who sits on the throne and from the anger of the Lamb! The terrible day of their anger is here and who can stand up against it?**

Throughout history, people have always tried to hide themselves when something terrible is happening on a certain part of the earth. Not everyone, but just the people, who are living in a place on the earth where something terrible is happening, that could kill the people who live there. This is something people are known for doing, when a terrible storm is coming. In the Midwest, where tornados are very popular and in the deep south where hurricanes are also very popular during a particular time of the year: people will run for shelter and hide from the storm. They will stay in a hidden shelter until the storm passes over. Some people on earth have better places to hide when disaster is coming.

Regular people take it upon themselves to build shelters they think would protect them from disastrous situations, like a storm. People on the earth who have power: they also have hidden shelter to run to if there is a disaster.

The shelters that powerful people have are designed to protect them from much more disastrous situations, like a storm. Powerful people have shelters that could protect them from nuclear disasters. Those shelters are so well built that they can stop someone from being killed from a nuclear disaster, whereas, many other people who are in less protective shelters, are killed in an instant. There are protective shelters here on this earth that are preserved for powerful people and those shelters are strong enough to protect anyone who is in them from extreme disastrous situations, like a nuclear war. So, there are different kinds of shelters, for different kinds of people: it all depends on who you are in the world.

Regular people have less powerful shelters, **hid themselves in the caves** and powerful people have more powerful shelters, **in the rocks of the mountains.** That is the way it is today and that was the way it was during the time of John. Regular people hid in caves when there was a storm and the people of power hid in mountains when there was a storm.

Today, many people are prepared to hide themselves in certain shelters that would protect them from disastrous situations and it was the same way for people who was here on this earth during the time of John: The only different is today, there are more people who have a place to hide to protect themselves from disaster situations. Today, there are many places here on earth where people can hide themselves from disastrous situations. Most people today live in houses that have basements. Today, there are many strong buildings where people can hide from a disastrous situation. People can even hide in their cars from some disastrous situation. Unlike, the time of John, there are many places here on this earth where people can hide themselves from disastrous situations.

Today, when people focus on a place of shelter, they are most like preparing themselves for a disastrous situation that have been known to humans for thousands of years and most likely it is a storm of some kind. Storms are disastrous situations that people are used to hiding from and there are a few other disastrous situations that people are used to hiding themselves from, but storms are the oldest, in human history. Today and even back during the time of John, people wouldn't think they would have to run for shelter from God and from the Lord Jesus. God and the Lord Jesus will be the last people, that people here on this earth would think they would have to hide from. So today, people don't think they would have to run for shelter from God and Jesus. But there will come a time on earth, when that will happen and when it happens, everyone on earth will know who they are running from. It will be made completely plain to them and just like people will run for shelter from a storm, they will try to run for shelter from God and Jesus.

When this happens, people will use the same shelters, they had prepared for other disastrous situations that they have a chance to hide themselves from, but when Jesus anger is more leased on the earth, than it is today, disastrous things will happen that never happened before and there won't be a place of shelter that could protect a person from it. During this time on earth, people will have such a strong desire to protect themselves from what the Lord Jesus will do to punish people; that in their minds, they will think, they will be able to find a place of shelter that would protect them from the wrath of Jesus, **and said to the mountains and rocks, Fall on us and hide us from the face of Him who sits on the throne and from the wrath of the Lamb.** But their thinking will be completely wrong, **for the great day of His wrath has come and who will be able to stand?**

In the 7th chapter and the 1st verse, in the King James version it says, **after these things I saw four angels standing at the four corners of the earth, holding the four winds of the earth, that the wind should not blow on the earth, on the sea, or on any tree.** In the English version it says, **after this I saw four angels standing at the four corners of the earth, holding back the four winds so that no wind should blow on the earth or the sea or against any tree.**

Storms move in different directions. Storms start in all direction. Sometime a storm can come from the east and sometime a storm can come from the west, but which ever direction a storm comes from, it has everything to do with the decision of God. God is the reason why there are storms on the earth and He uses Angels to move storms from one place on earth, to another place on earth.

The Angels of God are here on this earth, constantly causing the storms that all of us are familiar with, through the part of the news that forecasts the weather. The Angels of God are assigned to produce storms to show the anger of God.

Throughout history, God has used many storms to punish people who He was angry with. Actually, storms are produced by God through Angels; to punish people and that is why throughout the history of the weather, storms have left devasting destruction along its path.

Just before the return of Jesus, God will do away with storms and turn to another method to punish people that He never used before in human history. The wind is what God uses through Angels to move storms from one part of the earth to another part of the earth.

Whenever a storm comes or starts, believe me there is an Angel of God present, where ever the storm came from. After the Angel of God starts a storm, he moves with the storm he had started. A farmer, for an example, uses a tractor to plow the land he will use to plant seeds. As he is on the tractor, he is guiding the tractor by driving the tractor to where he wants the tractor to go; across the land he is plowing. As the tractor is plowing, where the farmer is driving, the plow on the back of the tractor is destroying the weed and anything else the farm doesn't want to grow with his harvest. So, the farmer will destroy what he doesn't want to grow with his harvest, as he drives the tractor over the area where the weeds are, that he wants to destroy: So, he is moving along with the tractor, as he is driving the tractor:

It is the same way with an Angle of God who creates a storm. The Angel is guiding the storm that he has created by moving with the storm he started. Just like the farmer; the Angel of God is guiding the storm where he wants that storm to destroy and get rid of the weeds, which are people who God doesn't want to live with His people.

God will continue to use storms to destroy people and the things people own, just before He is ready to send His Son Jesus to judge the world for their sins. Because God is the reason why storms exist: God is the person who can command His Angels to stop the existence of storms. So just as God created storms, He can also do away with storms. The first verse, in chapter seven, talks about God doing away with storms for a certain period of time, before He starts creating storming again, only for the purpose of what God created storm for and that is to destroy evil people and the things that evil people own. God will stop the existence of storm by commanding the Angel, who He uses, to create storms through the wind that Angels create. Storms are winds and it all depends on how strong the wind is, which will determine what classification a storm is. When the wind isn't blowing, then a storm isn't produced.

Although, a storm isn't produced, when the wind isn't blowing and because the wind isn't blowing, there is still an Angel of God at the location where storms usually begin, its just that the Angel is given a command not to stir up wind, to produce a storm, **after these things I saw four angels standing at the four corners of the earth, holding the four winds of the earth.**

The wind, that always produces storms, always starts in one of the four directions on the earth and people can distinguish, if a storm is about to happen, when the wind from the storm, blows on particular things, which is the earth, the sea and the trees. When the scripture says earth, that means everything on the earth the wind can blow against, to show people that a storm is about to happen or is happening at that particular time. The sea is also something else on the earth that will show that a storm is about to happen or is happening at a particular time and most trees also. God will show us that a storm will happen or a storm isn't going to happen by the blowing of the wind. If God allows the wind to blow, than He is showing us that a storm is approaching, but if God doesn't allow the wind to blow, He is showing us that a storm isn't approaching, **that the wind should not blow on the earth, on the sea, or on any tree.**

In the 2nd verse, in the King James version it says, **then I saw another angel ascending from the east, having the seal of the living God. And he cried with a loud voice to the four angels to whom it was granted to harm the earth and sea.** In the English version it says, **and I saw another angel coming up from the east with the seal of the living God. He called out in a loud voice to the four angels to whom God had given the power to damage the earth and the sea.**

Everything concerning God started and happened in the east before God revealed it to anyone else, in another part of the world. Adam and Eve were created in the east. When Noah built the ark; he built it in the east and when the water went down and the art rested on the earth; the ark rested in the east. When Abraham began to have faith in God that happened in the east. King David existed in the east. Jesus existed in the east. Everything concerning God started in the east, then it went to other parts of the world. The stories of the holy people, that I just mentioned, started in the east, then after that, people all over the world heard about these holy and beautiful people. So, like I said, everything concerning God started in the east, then it went to other parts of the world.

As a result, there have always been people all over the world who believed, learned and obeyed the true and living God, but the belief, the learning and the obedience to God started in the east. The promise land to be exact.

Because everything concerning God started in the east, that is the reason why the Angel of God, that is mentioned, in the second verse, of the seventh chapter, is located in the east and he will represent only the people in the promise land who will be faithful to God at the time of John's vision, **then I saw another angel ascending from the east.** The reason why this Angel will be located in the east; in the promise land to be exact, is because all of the things of God here on this earth started in the east. When it says, "ascending" in the second verse, of chapter seven, it means that the Angel of God is ready to do what God had assign for him to do here on this earth and that is to offer and give protection only to the people who will live in the promise, who are faithful to God. The seal, the Angel will have, is the guarantee that everyone who is faithful to God in the promise land, during the time of John's vision; they won't be harmed from what is about to happen because of a great storm that will swept through the whole earth, **having the seal of the living God.**

The people who will be faithful to God, during the time this verse points to, will be located only in the east; in the promise land. It will be one hundred and forty-four thousand Jews.

Some Angels have more power than others. Some Angels give orders to other Angels. Some Angels are very demanding towards other Angels they give orders to. Not because the Angels, who are giving the orders, think the other Angel who will receive the orders, don't want to obey him, but the reason why Angels are sometime demanding when they give orders to other Angels, is because the Angel who is receiving the orders, have a very large number of other Angels helping him, which will be the case in this situation, **and he cried with a loud voice.**

Sometime Angels do things on their own and sometime they are helped by a very large number of other Angels. When destruction is massive, which is what is about to happen, then one Angel, that is in charge, is assisted by a very large number of other Angels. The Angel who is giving a particular command, isn't only heard by the other Angel he is giving a command to, but the very large number of other Angels that will assist him, will also here the command, **to the four angels.**

In the second verse, which is the verse where the command will be began, but not yet given, to the four Angels and to the assisting Angels, not to harm the earth and the sea at the moment by giving a command not to produce any storms, **to whom it was granted to harm the earth and sea.**

In the 3rd verse, in the King James version it says saying, **do not harm the earth, the sea or the trees till we have sealed the servants of our God on their foreheads.** In the English version it says, **the angel said, do not harm the earth and the sea or the trees, until we mark the servants of our God with a seal on their foreheads.**

The word forehead, in this verse, represents the mind. It is through the mind that a person sins because it is in the mind were sin starts. Because the mind, is the place in the body where sin starts, a person has to have their minds changed by the Holy Spirit before they are able to do, the good deeds that only a person can do, who has received power from God to do so. A person who is faithful to God has a changed mind, which the Apostle Paul calls, "a renewed mind." When a person's mind is renewed, which means changed, a seal is placed on their forehead by the Holy Spirit today, but during the time of this scripture, the seal of God will be placed on a person who is faithful to God by Angels, rather than by the Holy Spirit.

Why? Because at this time, the Holy Spirit won't be here on this earth: He will be in God's Kingdom with God and Jesus.

During the time of John and even today, a person who has a changed mind, is the person who is faithful to God. Everyone who is faithful to God is protected by God and for that reason, no one or thing is able to harm them. Just like the Holy Spirit can protect a person, an Angel of God has the power to protect a person from the things that are harmful. The results of a changed mind is the protection of God. Everyone who is faithful to God, during the time this verse points to, will receive protection from God through the Angels of God. So if an Angel of God protects a person before something harmful happens, then that is the person who will be unharmed from anything that is harmful that is about to happen, **do not harm the earth, the sea or the trees till we have sealed the servants of our God on their foreheads.**

In the 4th verse, in the King James version it says, **and I heard the number of those who were sealed. One hundred and forty-four thousand of all the tribes of the children of Israel were sealed.**

In the 5th verse, in the King James version, which is connected to the 4th verse, it says:

5 of the tribe of Judah twelve
    thousand were sealed;
  of the tribe of Reuben twelve
    thousand were sealed;
  of the tribe of Gad twelve
    thousand were sealed;
6 of the tribe of Asher twelve
    thousand were sealed;
  of the tribe of Naphtali twelve
    thousand were sealed;
  of the tribe of Manasseh twelve
    thousand were sealed;
7 of the tribe of Simeon twelve
    thousand were sealed;
  of the tribe of Levi twelve
    thousand were sealed;
  of the tribe of Issachar twelve
    thousand were sealed;
8 of the tribe of Zebulun twelve
    thousand were sealed;
  of the tribe of Joseph twelve
    thousand were sealed;
  of the tribe of Benjamin twelve
    thousand were sealed.

If a person is a believer and they are holy in the eyes of God, Jesus through the Holy Spirit, will tell that person a lot of things and the things the Holy Spirit will tell them, will be in specific detail. So, exactly what the Holy Spirit tells them, that is exactly the way it will be. The Holy Spirit will talk to people, just like people talk to people, but in a language that is spiritual because the Holy Spirit talks only to the hearts of people and the hearts of people is called, "their spirit." Our spirit, is a spirit, that is just like the Holy Spirit, the only difference is, "the Holy Spirit" is "Divine" because He is God. The Holy Spirit: He is the only Spirit, who can protect a person from all harm and danger. That is something the Holy Spirit has done since the creation of Man.

If a person is protected by the Holy Spirit, then that protection is in the form of a seal that can't be seen by the naked eye, but it can be seen by a person who has received it, through the protection they will notice in their lives, when they will begin to see how they are able to avoid many dangerous situations without being harmed; whereas, other people who have experienced the same situations are completely destroyed.

The Holy Spirit told John: The number of people who would be protected on this earth, during the time this verse points to. The Holy Spirit also told John, the kind of people, those people would be by the names of the tribes that was given to him by the Holy Spirit, **and I heard the number of those who were sealed. One hundred and forty-four thousand of all the tribes of the children of Israel were sealed.**

The people in the promise land who will be protected by God will be the children of Israel. This isn't a coincidence. The reason God will allowed for this to happen this way is because; like I told you earlier, everything that has to do with God: It started in the east; in the promise land and that is where it all has to end; in the promise land. It is almost the end of time this verse is pointing to. Sometime things have to end where they start. The first people who were the children of God were located in the east; in the promise land and that is why during this time, the only people who will be faithful to God, will be in the promise land, which is where the one hundred and forty-four thousand will be. The promise land is where the children of God first existed here on this earth and it will be the last place on this earth they will be. I would never think that one day on this earth there would be only one place where God's children would be, but that will happen.

In the 9th verse, in the King James version it says, **after these things I looked and behold, a great multitude which no one could number, of all nations, tribes, peoples and tongues, standing before the throne and behold the Lamb, clothed with white robes, with palm branches in their hands.** In the English version it says, **after this I looked and there was an enormous crowd – no one could count all the people! They were from every race, tribe, nation and language and they stood in front of the throne and of the Lamb, dressed in white robes and holding palm branches in their hands.**

John received revelation from the Holy Spirit; piece by piece, concerning the things that would happen near the end of the world. After, the Holy Spirit showed John one thing, He showed John something else, **after these things I looked and behold**. It doesn't have to be that many people or that many of anything, before a person will lose their count. It is easier to count people or anything that is in small numbers, but when the numbers start increasing, then it is very easy for a person to lose track of what they are counting, **a great multitude which no one could number.**

Compared to the number of people in Heaven, to the number of people who came here on this earth from the time of Adam, to the present time, the number of people in Heaven is very small, but large in number, if those people aren't match to any other number, except themselves.

People have gone to Heaven ever since the creation of Man. People have gone to Heaven from the time of Adam, to the period of time this verse mentions. There isn't just one group of people in Heaven, there are many different groups of people in Heaven. So, in other words, not only is there white people in Heaven, but there are black people in Heaven also. There are some Chinese people in Heaven. There are some Latin people in Heaven. There are some Indians in Heaven. There are all kinds of different people in Heaven from all nationalities and there will be a lot of people in Heaven during the time of this verse and there is also a lot of people in Heaven today, **a great multitude which no one could number, of all nations, tribes, peoples and tongues.**

When souls go to Heaven; their souls are placed under the altar of God, but during a special occasion in God's Kingdom, those same souls that are under the altar of God are brought from underneath the altar and placed in front of God's throne.

This is always a celebration of commemorating the salvation that people have received from Jesus, through the Holy Spirit, when they became saved on this earth. This kind of celebration happens often in the Kingdom of God, especially, when a large number of people make it into God's Kingdom at the same time. The celebration was for the one hundred and forty-four thousand Jews who made it into Heaven about the same time. When a person enters into God's Kingdom; after they leave this earth, the people in God's Kingdom who celebrates the victory of that person, is the Father, Jesus, the twenty four elders and the Cherubim and Seraphim Angels, but when a large number of people enter into God's Kingdom at the same time, then the souls who are underneath God's altar; they participate in the celebration as well. This celebration always happens in front of God where He rules everything through Jesus and Jesus is also the person who everyone honors along with the Father because a person receives salvation on this earth by the Father, through Jesus, **standing before the throne and behold the Lamb.**

When a person is pure in the heart, good deeds are what other people are able to see, **clothed.** I said this earlier in this writing, people who are faithful to God, are people who are viewed by God as being a priest, who are represented by the color white because white is the color that represents purification, which is when a person's soul isn't mixed with sin. A person whose heart is pure, is justified by God as a priest. A priest in the Old Testament days was a man who was expected to get a prayer through to God; in the same way, a person who is identified by God as a priest can get a prayer through to God, **with white robes.**

If a person is truly faithful to God, there is nothing or no other person who can stop them from being obedient to God, **with palm branches in their hands.** Those kinds of people, are like palm branches because back during the time of John, a palm tree in the promise land was stronger than any other tree. During a very powerful wind storm, other trees would snap when the wind would blow against them, but the palm tree always endured. Why? Because the palm tree was able to bend away from the wind, whereas, the other tree couldn't bend, so as a result, the tree would snap. In the same way, a person who is faithful to God, will bend away from the influence of sin when ever the devil uses sin to try and turn them away from God. So, a person who is faithful to God will continue to endure and remain faithful to God after being tempted by the devil through sin.

The one hundred and forty-four thousand were the people who John saw in the nineth verse, being congratulated in Heaven by everyone who made it into Heaven before they did.

In the 10th verse, in the King James version it says, **and crying out with a loud voice, saying, Salvation belongs to our God who sits on the throne and to the Lamb.** In the English version it says, **they called out in a loud voice: Salvation comes from our God, who sits on the throne and from the Lamb!"**

It means something different when an Angel cries out with a loud voice, then when a person's soul cries out to God, when a person's soul is in Heaven. When someone cries out with a loud voice, that usually means that a person is trying to get another person's attention for a particular reason or it can also mean that a person wants to say something with very strong emotion. When an Angel or a person cries out with a very strong emotion in a scripture, it can mean different things, it all depends on how the scripture is worded. In this scripture, many souls in Heaven came together to celebrate the arrival of the souls of many people who remain faithful to God under very difficult circumstances on earth.

The people who were being celebrated for their arrival in the Kingdom of God were the one hundred and forty-four thousand, who received protection from God, when God's anger had influence Him to destroy many people by a severe storm that He caused to swept across the world. The only people who were saved from destruction were the one hundred and forty-four thousand.

The one hundred and forty-four thousand were saved because they had received salvation in their souls that comes from God. The salvation that comes from God is the salvation that offers two things. One: The salvation that comes from Gods offers deliverance from sin and two: It offers protection from anything that is able to harm a person here on this earth. It is a very great blessing from God when a person is able to receive the salvation that comes from God and any person or group of people who receives the salvation that comes from God, is more than worth to be praised by other people, who have received the salvation of God and they are also worth of receiving the praise that comes from God and Jesus, who is the Lamb.

When the souls of those who were already in God's Kingdom; praised the souls of those who had arrived, which were the one hundred and forty-four thousand; they praise the souls of the one hundred and forty-one thousand with very strong emotions, **and crying out with a loud voice.**

When the souls of those who were already in Heaven, when the one hundred and forty-four thousand souls had arrived, they gave God and Jesus complete credit for the salvation the one hundred and forty-four thousand souls had received, when they were here on this earth, before they died, **saying, Salvation belongs to our God who sits on the throne and to the Lamb.**

In the 11th verse, in the King James version it says, **all the angels stood around the throne and the elders and the four living creatures and fell on their faces before the throne and worshiped God.** In the English version it says, **all the angels stood around the throne, the elders and the four living creatures. Then they threw themselves face downward in front of the throne and worshiped God.**

When John saw this celebration take place, that actually didn't happen yet, he saw three groups of people in this part of his vision. He saw all of God Angels, the elders and the four highest Angels that represent the four creatures. There are some discussions about who the twenty-four elders are in the Kingdom of God. I heard this preacher on this religious program sometime ago in the past; talk briefly about the twenty-four elders and he said that no one knows exactly who the twenty-four elders are. Well, this is who those twenty-four elders are, who are around God's throne.

Now, I don't know actually who all of them are, but I know who some of them are. The twenty-four elders are the people who were chosen by God when they were here on this earth and no more will be added to the souls of those who were chosen by God to be the twenty-four elders, so in other words, there won't be a twenty-fifth elder. Some of the twenty-four elders are: Adam who was the first man and don't be surprised when I say Adam because Adam went to Heaven and you will find that in the twelfth chapter of Revelation. Noah, Abraham, Isaac, Jacob, Joseph, Moses, Joshua, David, Elijah, Elisha, Job, Isaiah, Jeremiah, Ezekiel, Daniel, Peter, the Apostle Paul, James, John, and four more men.

Like I said, in this part of John's vision, he saw three groups of people; all of God's Angels, the elders and the four highest Angels that represent the four creatures. When a celebration takes place in God's Kingdom for the salvation that a person or a group of people have received in their souls, when they were here on this earth, all of God's Angel in Heaven celebrate along with the twenty-four elders. When a person or group of people receive salvation in their souls here on earth, all of God's Angels and the twenty-four elders celebrate, but when there is a person or group of people on this earth during a particular time period on this earth, who has received salvation, it is very special to the Angels of God and to the twenty-four elders.

The reason why the salvation of the one hundred and forty-four thousand is special, out of everyone who has received salvation on this earth, is because during this time in Jewish history, everyone in the world will go against Jerusalem, which is where all of these Jews will be located. As a result, every country in the world will turn against the promise land because of the one hundred and forty-four thousand. During this time, the last anti-christ will take over the whole world, except, for Jerusalem and because of Jerusalem, the last anti-christ couldn't defeat the entire promise land, which was something that no king in the whole world could do, during the time when King David was King of the promise land through Jerusalem and because of King David's throne is the reason why God sent His Son Jesus. Because the one hundred and forty-four thousand was in Jerusalem, during this special time for God, is the reason why the salvation of the one hundred and forty-four thousand will be very special in Heaven, **all the angels stood around the throne and the elders and the four living creatures**.

During the time of John, a king was the person every one obeyed and respected; even when the king wasn't sitting on his throne in front of people. But the king's position was much more respected when the king was seen sitting on his throne. During the time of John, people always obeyed and respected the king, but there was something about the king's position when he was seen sitting on his throne in front of others, but even when he wasn't sitting on his throne, he was obeyed and respected. There was something very powerful about the king's position as being king when he was seen sitting on his throne.

The king's position was seen a lot more when he was seen sitting on his throne, than when he wasn't seen sitting on his throne. When the king was seen sitting on his throne, then everyone who seen him and even those who didn't see him, knew there was something very, very, very, important that the king already did or there was something the king was preparing to do.

As a result, the people who were before the king, when he was sitting on his throne; they would offer to submit themselves to the king and they would do that by bowing their face down to the ground where the king's throne was.

In the same way, every being in Heaven obeys and respects God's position as being King. But when there is something that is very, very, very, important that God has already done or there is something that God was preparing to do: Every being in His Kingdom will offer to submit themselves to God, **then they threw themselves face downward in front of the throne and worshiped God.** Every being in Heaven obeys and respect God, but every being offers submission when God has already done something or when He is prepared to do something.

What did God do, that influenced every being in Heaven to recognize God's position as King, which cause them to offer submission to God? What God did on behalf of King David and Jesus, which is when He allowed for Jerusalem to stand against the last anti-christ and the whole world, just before He sent His Son Jesus to judge the world.

In the 12th verse, in the King James version it says, **saying: Amen! Blessing and glory and wisdom, Thanksgiving and honor and power and might, Be to our God forever and ever. Amen.**

There are somethings that God only wants His people to know and there are somethings that God wants ever one to know. Everyone is supposed to know who the real God is and the real God, is the God who is the only Father. The Father of the Lord Jesus: He is the real and only God. God is the one who owns everything, regardless, if people believe that or not. God doesn't just want people to know that He own everything. God especially wants people to know that what He gives to people is something He will own forever, **blessing and glory and wisdom** and something God receives from His people, **Thanksgiving and honor** and something He will have, **and power and might** forever and all of these spiritual things belongs to God forever, **be to our God forever and ever.**

This is something that God what's everyone to know, **Amen.** These spiritual things will belong to God until the old universe disappears, **forever** and for eternity, **and ever.**

In the 13th verse, in the King James version it says, **then one of the elders answered, saying to me, who are these arrayed in white robes and where did they come from?**

The subject is still: The one hundred and forty-four thousand and because the subject is still the one hundred and forty-four thousand, it is the reason why one of the elders, whose name isn't mentioned; asked John a question concerning the one hundred and forty-four thousand. The Angels and souls who are in the Kingdom of God know much more then what we do because they are given supernatural power that belongs to the Kingdom of God, but they are capable of sharing supernatural information to the people who are here on this earth. When a person is truly saved in their souls by the Holy Spirit, they are able to receive all power, but not all knowledge.

The knowledge a person receives who is truly saved here on this earth is limited, compared to the knowledge the souls have who entered into the Kingdom of God after they had died here on this earth. The knowledge, beings have in the Kingdom of God, is far beyond the knowledge, that saved people have received here on this earth from the Holy Spirit. Matter of fact, there are somethings we wouldn't receive an answer about, unless we receive in from one of the beings who are in God's Kingdom.

Beings, as you know, are people who are alive some where and there are many Angels and souls who are alive in God's Kingdom. When a being, in God's Kingdom; asks a person a question who is saved here on this earth; they ask that person a question for a reason and it is always a good reason because a person who is truly saved here on this earth and saved in God's Kingdom; they don't ask anyone a question for silly purposes because everyone who is truly saved is mature like Jesus, so foolishness is something they don't become involved with and asking a person a question for no reason is foolishness.

We can lose focus even in a vision that we receive from God, just like we can lose focus in a conversation we have on this earth. A vision is a conversation between God and a person and because it is a vision, it is a conversation between God and a person, so someone can lose focus in a vision, just like they can in a conversation here on this earth. People lose focus in a conversation when the conversation is long and the vision John had was very long and we can see that through the length of Revelation. John lost a little focus of the vision, at this point in the vision. So, one of the elders had to bring his focus towards the vision back on track.

For a very short moment, John forgot who the one hundred and forty-four thousand souls were and where they came from and that is what the one elder reminded him of, which is what John had forgot, **then one of the elders answered, saying to me, Who are these arrayed in white robes and where did they come from?**

In the 14th verse, in the King James version is says, **and I said to him, "Sir, you know." So he said to me, These are the ones who come out of the great tribulation and washed their robes and made them white in the blood of the Lamb.** In the English version it says, **I don't know, sir. You do, "I answered. He said to me, "These are the people who died in the great tribulation. They have washed their robes and made them white with the blood of the Lamb.**

At this moment in the vision, John had forgotten who the one hundred and forty-four thousand were and he forgot where they came from, **I don't know, sir. You do, "I answered.**

The last anti-christ will take over the whole world very easy and every country in the world will place themselves under his power: so, the last anti-christ will rule the whole world during this time in John's vision.

During this time in history, every country will be under the power of the anti-christ, except, for Jerusalem and the promise land. The anti-christ who will be a Muslim in Iraq, will try to do every thing he can military to bring Jerusalem and the promise land under his power and he will try to do this from Iraq, which he had great success in doing, to all other countries. Out of frustration, he will go to Jerusalem with his army and continue the attack that he started towards Jerusalem from Iraq.

When the last anti-christ arrive in Jerusalem, he will not only go through Jerusalem killing Jews, but he will go through the entire promise land killing other Jews who are outside of Jerusalem, **these are the ones who come out of the great tribulation.** It is called, "the awful horror" in the twenty fourth chapter; starting at the fifteenth verse, in the book, "according to the Gospel of Matthew." This is why it says, in one of the scriptures in Psalms, "pray for Jerusalem."

Every person who is a believer has a robe in the eyes of God and because they have a robe in the eyes of God, although, they aren't holy yet; they are considered by God as a priest, but they are a priest who can't enter into the most holy place, but they can enter into the holy place.

The most holy place was in the tent that God told Moses to build, where only the high priest had the authority to go because he was acceptable to God, but the other priests were only allowed in the holy place, which was outside of the most holy place. The tent was a copy of the Kingdom of God. The most holy place in the tent represented the place in God's Kingdom where the throne of God is and the presents of the Lamb. The holy place in the tent represented the place in God's Kingdom where all the Angels are who are under the power of Jesus through the Cherubim and Seraphim Angels.

People who are believers, but aren't holy yet: they have the chance to enter into the Kingdom of God for information, but they aren't allowed into the Kingdom throne, of God Kingdom, until they become holy. The one hundred and forty-four thousand became believers and after they became believers, they became holy like everyone else who becomes holy. A person has to become a believer before they are holy. When a person becomes a believer and then becomes holy, then they are a priest in the eyes of God, **and washed their robes.**

When a person becomes holy, then they become pure and the only way a person can become pure, is because of what Jesus did on the cross, which represents the blood of Jesus.

Why does the crucifixion of Jesus makes a person pure, "(white)" because the crucifixion of Jesus is how a person can receive power from the Holy Spirit to turn from sin, "to stop sinning" then after that, a person will be raised to life by the Holy Spirit, which means, receive power to live holy, which is what the resurrection of Jesus represents. So, a person become pure in heart through the crucifixion of Jesus, **and made them white in the blood of the Lamb.** The one hundred and forty-four thousand experienced the same thing that everyone else experiences, who made a transformation from being a sinner, to being holy. The one hundred and forty-four thousand were protected at one time, when a lot of people were killed here on this earth by a very fierce storm that swept across the world, but eventually, they were killed for Jesus sake. Like everyone else, the one hundred and forty-four thousand received salvation and then they were made holy.

In the 15th verse, in the King James version it says, **therefore they are before the throne of God and serve Him day and night in His temple. And He who sits on the throne will dwell among them.** In the English version it says, **that is why they stand before God's throne and serve Him day and night in His temple. And He who sits on the throne will give them shelter.**

There were a lot of people who received salvation from the Spirit of God on this earth. The one hundred and forty-four thousand, weren't the only people who received salvation from God. So as a result, all of the people who had received salvation from God when they were here on this earth, has a chance to stand before God's throne and they stand before God's throne sometime, but not all the time. All the souls of the people who entered into God's Kingdom are underneath the altar of God.

Under the altar of God, is where all the people souls are located in the Kingdom of God, but the souls of the one hundred and forty-four thousand wouldn't be located underneath the altar of God; their souls will be before God's throne all the time, **therefore they are before the throne of God and serve Him day and night in His temple.** Why? Like I said earlier because of what happened concerning the one hundred and forty-four thousand when they were here on this earth. What happened and the way it happened because they had received salvation from God, is something that no one has experienced on this earth who was saved.

There are many places in God's Kingdom, but there is only one place where God rules and that is the place in His Kingdom where His throne is located, which is the same place where Jesus is, who is, "the Son of God."

This place inside God's Kingdom is the place where the worship of God happens from all the spiritual beings that exist in Heaven and this place is called, "God's temple." Just like on this earth, there are many places where believers are located, but the place where all of them worshipped God on this earth, during the time of John, was in the temple, not in the synagogue. In the same way, out of all the places in God's Kingdom, there is only one place where God is worshipped and that is in the "temple of God." Although, throughout God's Kingdom, there are Angels everywhere, but they all meet in God's temple to worship God.

Until Jesus returns, the only people who will have a place to dwell before God's throne, which is located inside His temple, are the one hundred and forty-four thousand, **and He who sits on the throne will dwell among them.** All the other souls who made it to Heaven are underneath the altar of God.

In the 16th verse, in the King James version it says, **they shall neither hunger anymore nor thirst anymore; the sun shall not strike them, nor any heat.** In the English version is says, **never again will they hunger or thirst; neither sun nor any scorching heat will burn them.**

Everyone who has received salvation from the Spirit of God, when they were here on this earth, had a strong desire to go to Heaven when they die, but the one hundred and forty-four thousand had the strongest desire to go to Heaven, then any other person who had received salvation here on this earth, the same as they did, **they shall neither hunger anymore nor thirst anymore.**

Everyone who has received salvation from the Spirit of God on this earth, went through persecution and even experienced persecution that lead to their death, but the one hundred and forty-four thousand experienced a kind of persecution that no other person who has received salvation, had ever experienced, **the sun shall not strike them, nor any heat.** Throughout Christian history, there has never been a time when a large number of believers were killed at once for the sake of God and Jesus; like the amount of the one hundred and forty-four thousand. There had been many believers who had been persecuted at the same time or around the same time, but there has never been a large amount killed at one time, like the one hundred and forty-four thousand.

In the 17th verse, in the King James version it says, **for the Lamb who is in the midst of the throne will shepherd them and lead them to living fountains of water. And God will wipe away every tear from their eyes.**

In the English version it says, **because the Lamb, who is in the center of the throne, will be their shepherd and He will guide them to springs of life-giving water. And God will wipe away every tear from their eyes.**

Jesus is the only person who makes it possible to have a relationship with the Father. Before Jesus was crucified and resurrected and before He sent back the Holy Spirit; Jesus as always sat at the right side of God, but when Jesus sent back the Holy Spirit; after His crucifixion and resurrection, Jesus place in God's Kingdom wasn't just at the right side of God; now His place in God's Kingdom is also in the center of God's throne, which means that Jesus is the one who is between God and every one else who is in God's Kingdom and everyone who is here on this earth who has received salvation, **because the Lamb, who is in the center of the throne.** The center of anything, has something on one side and something else on the other side.

If there is something in between what is on one side and what is on the other side, then that is what is in between. In the same way, in God's temple, there is a person on one side and there is a group of people on the other side and someone in the middle. In God temple; God is on one side and everyone else is on the other side and Jesus is in between.

Jesus is the shepherd to everyone who has received salvation and as a shepherd, Jesus teaches people the things they need to do, to please the Father and as a result, they are given an important position in God's Kingdom, but the one hundred and forty-four thousand will have a position in God's Kingdom that will be higher, then every position that anyone has or will have in the Kingdom of God, when the Kingdom of God will be brought down to where the earth is now, **will be their shepherd.**

Everyone who has received salvation from the Spirit of God is guided to springs of life-giving water, but the one hundred and forty-four thousand will go from the spiritual position, they all had on this earth, as being children of God, to a position that will be higher then the position that anyone will have in the Kingdom of God, **and He will guide them to springs of life-giving water.** Springs of life-giving water means this. A spring goes from one place to another, when the water in a spring travels from one place to another. In the same way, a person who has received salvation, after being a sinner, will travel from one place to another **spring.** The person was able to travel from being a sinner, to being saved because of the water that will make it possible for a person to live the life that God wants them to live, **life-giving water.**

The water is the Holy Word of God, which is the Holy Bible and the Holy Bible will make it possible for a person to travel from being a sinner, to being saved. In the same way, the one hundred and forty-four thousand will travel from the spiritual position they will have here on this earth, as children of God, to the highest position in God's Kingdom that will be on the new earth.

Everyone who has received salvation from the Spirit of God, is free from sorrow and is no longer in an emotional state of crying, but the one hundred and forty-four thousand will receive a kind of joy that no one else in the Kingdom of God will experience. On the new earth, everyone will still have emotions, but they will be emotions of joy. Everyone on the new earth will be happy they made it to the Kingdom of God, but the one hundred and forty-four thousand will be the happiest out of everyone, **and God will wipe away every tear from their eyes.**

In the 8th chapter and the 1st verse, in the King James version it says, **when He opened the seventh seal, there was silence in Heaven for about an half and hour.**

All of God's Angels respect Him because He is God. There are times in God's Kingdom when all of God's Angels, are completely quiet because of the respect they have for something that God is getting ready to do at the present time.

It's kind of like church service. Before the preacher preaches his message, there is a lot of noise in church, but when the preacher gets up to preach his message; then there is silence throughout the church and no one is allowed to make any noise until the preach finishes his message and the people in the church do that out of respect for the preacher. That is the same way it is in the Kingdom God. All the Angels of God, along with the souls who are in Heaven, will silence themselves because of something that God is getting ready to do, that is very important to God and everyone is silenced for a certain period of time. Before God does something here on this earth, He make preparations to do what He plans to do.

Just like, the preacher in church prepares the end of the service through his preaching because in most churches after the preacher preaches, then what follows is the end of the service. What God was making preparations for, concerning the coming of Jesus, was done in the opening of the seventh seal. What God was preparing in the opening of the seventh seal would end the whole universe, just as the preaching of the preacher would end the entire church service.

The end of the universe, which was prepared by the opening of the seventh seal, which would be very important to God, is the reason why there was silence in the opening of the seventh seal, **when He opened the seventh seal, there was silence in Heaven.**

What God did, as He made preparation to do through Jesus what He planned to do, which would end the universe; would last for a half an hour in earthly time, **for about an half and hour.**

In the 2nd verse, in the King James version it says, **and I saw the seven angels who stand before God and to them were given seven trumpets.**

The Angels of God are the spiritual being in Heaven that God uses to do the work that He wants done here on this earth and the Angels of God are given a command to do something through Jesus. Back during the time of John, every time a trumpet was blown, it was a sign for the people to get ready and prepare themselves for something that was going to happen and more so, in the Old Testament days, especially, from Moses, up to the time of Elijah.

In the same way, the Angels of God are commanded to prepare themselves every time God blows a spiritual trumpet in Heaven through Jesus. There are times when God doesn't use Jesus to blow the trumpet, but He commands Jesus to give His trumpet to His Angels and they are the ones who are assigned by God, through Jesus, to blow the trumpet of God, which is when the Angels of God will prepare the other Angels, for something that God wants them to do on this earth, just like the trumpets were blown to prepare the people for what was going to happen. The things that God wants to happen here on this earth because of the breaking of the seventh seal, He will give only seven Angels the authority, through Jesus, to prepare other Angels for what God wants to do here on this earth and those seven Angels are the Seraphims. Sometime or a lot of the time, the Seraphim Angels are given authority to command other Angels to assist them in something that God want to do here on this earth and those other Angels are expected to obey, **and I saw the seven angels who stand before God and to them were given seven trumpets.**

In the 3rd verse, in the King James version it says, **then another angel, having a golden censer, came and stood at the altar. He was given much incense, that he should offer it with the prayers of all the saints upon the golden altar which was before the throne.** In the English version it says, **another angel, who had a gold incense container, came and stood at the altar. He was given a lot of incense to add to the prayers of all God's people and to offer it on the gold altar that stands before the throne.**

Just like there are burning incense today, there were burning incense during the time of John. In the Kingdom of God, an incense represents the prayers of those who are holy in the eyes of God and the smoke from the incense represent the prayers that goes up to God, from the people who are holy. If you would light an incense and pay close attention to the smoke of the incense, as the incense begins to burn; you will see the smoke of the incense go up and that is why the incense, along with the smoke, represent the prayers that are prayed by holy people that are answered by God.

Most of the time, the Angel that is before God's throne will take a gold incense container and he would put the prayers of the people who are holy in a gold incense container. Then the Angel would offer those prayers to God and God would answer those prayers by doing what those prayers requested God to do. But that will change for a brief moment, during the time, that the third verse point to. For a brief moment, the golden incense container wasn't used to offer prayers to God, from people who are holy: The gold container will be used to pour God's anger down to this earth on people who God would be angry with because they were mistreating Gods people, **another angel, who had a gold incense container, came and stood at the altar.**

Sometime God will add something to the prayer request of those who pray to Him who are holy and what God adds to their prayer request is completely connected to what those holy people ask God for. When God adds something to the prayer request of the people, who are holy; the Angel who is at the altar of God, will give what God wants those people to have, along with what they have already asked God to give them in prayer, **he was given a lot of incense to add to the prayers of all God's people** The incenses that comes from God, are different from the incenses that comes from God's holy people. The incenses of God, are the things that God adds to the prayer request that are made to God by His people, which God will answer. All of the prayers that are answered by God, are prayers that make it to God's altar, where they are answered, which is the reason why the Angel offers it on the altar of God, **and to offer it on the gold altar that stands before the throne.**

In the 4th verse, in the King James version it says, **and the smoke of the incense, with the prayers of the saints, ascended before God from the angel's hand.** In the English version it says, **the smoke of the burning incense went up with the prayers of God's people from the hands of the angel standing before God.**

These are the steps that are taken of the prayers that are prayed by God's holy people. When the prayers of God holy people are prayed to God, those prayers will go up to God from this earth. When those prayers reach God's Kingdom, the Angel that is before God's altar will take those prayers and offer those prayers on the altar that is before God. As those prayers are offered, the prayers will go to God from the Angel, then God will answer those prayers and the answer of those prayers will go back to the people by that Angel, but if there is something that God wants to add or in other words, give with the prayers that He will answer, than something else will be given to those people, along with what they already had asked God for. Then the Angel will give to those people what they had already ask God for, along with what God wants to give them, with what they wanted from God, **the smoke of the burning incense went up with the prayers of God's people from the hands of the angel standing before God.**

In the 5th verse, in the King James version it says, **then the angel took the censer, filled it with fire from the altar and threw it to the earth. And there were noises, thunderings, lightenings and an earthquake.** In the English version it says, **then the angel took the incense container, filled it with fire from the altar and threw it on the earth. There were rumbling and peals of thunder, flashes of lightning and an earthquake.**

During the time, that this part of John's vision point to in this verse, there was something that God's holy people were asking God for here on this earth and that was for God to protect them from the people who was also here on this earth, who were mistreating them and God answered their prayers by doing something, along with what they had asked Him for. What God did, along with what they had asked God to do, which was to protect them: Is God killed the people, that His people had asked Him to protect them from, **then the angel took the censer, filled it with fire from the altar and threw it to the earth.**

Whenever there is rumbling and peals of thunder, flashes of lightning and an earthquake, God is angry at a group of people because of something those people are going that God isn't pleased with. Throughout human history, God's anger was always the reason for rumbling and peals of thunder, flashes of lightning and earthquakes. In most cases, punishment is done by God, to those who God is angry with, as a result of rumbling and peals of thunder, flashes of lightning and earthquakes.

The rumbling and peals of thunder, flashes of lightning and earthquakes are things that happens before God punishes people because of His anger and the rumbling and peals of thunder, flashes of lightning and earthquakes are things that happens after God's punishes people because of His anger and that was what many people heard here on this earth when God punished the people who were mistreating God people, during the time, that this part of John's vision points to, **there were rumbling and peals of thunder, flashes of lightning and an earthquake.**

Now, don't get confused, this happened after the existence of the one hundred and forty-four thousand. The existence of the one hundred and forty-four thousand was the sixth seal; these people existed here on this earth in the seventh seal. During the time of the one hundred and forty four thousand; the only people who were obedient to God, were located in Jerusalem and a few others were located in parts of the promise land outside of Jerusalem, but when God's people; who are mentioned in the fifth verse; were here on this earth, there were people all over the earth who were obedient to God, but there were only a few. A lot less in number, then the one hundred and forty-four thousand.

Made in United States
Orlando, FL
09 August 2023

35826359R20059